LEGO® Friends™

Friendship Fun written by Olivia London

LB

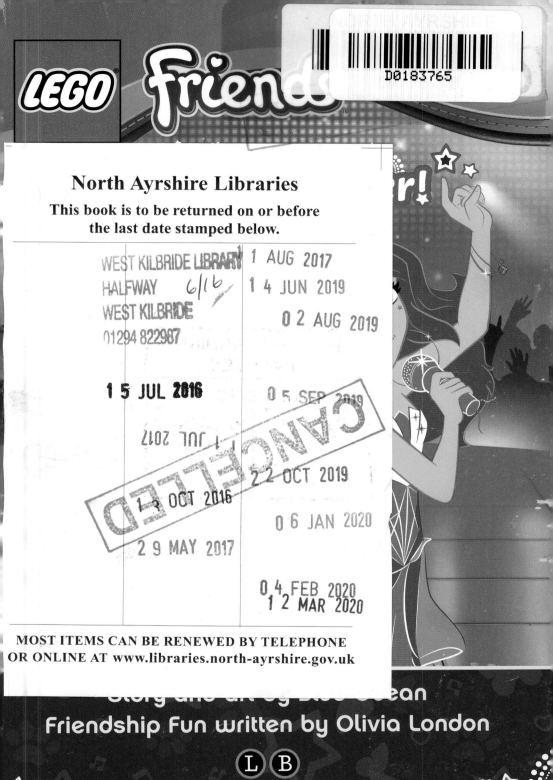

Little, Brown Books for Young Readers
www.lbkids.co.uk

LITTLE, BROWN BOOKS FOR YOUNG READERS

First published in the United States in 2016 by Little, Brown and Company
This edition published in Great Britain in 2016 by Hodder and Stoughton

1 3 5 7 9 10 8 6 4 2

Stories written by Marisa Reinelt
Pencils and inks by Fernando Dominguez and Carlos Arroyo
Colors by Miriam Hidalgo and Oriol San Julian

A CIP catalogue record for this book is available from the British Library.

ISBN 978-1-51020-062-3

Printed in the United States

Little, Brown Books for Young Readers
An imprint of
Hachette Children's Group
Part of Hodder and Stoughton
Carmelite House
50 Victoria Embankment
London EC4Y 0DZ

An Hachette UK Company
www.hachette.co.uk

www.hachettechildrens.co.uk

Welcome to Heartlake City

Heartlake City is the home of LEGO Friends, five very different and very talented girls who are best friends. The city is centered around a heart-shaped lake (hence the name!), located directly between a beach and a mountain range. This location makes it perfect for all kinds of outdoor activities like flying, horse riding, dolphin observing, and more! The city itself is home to a mall, a café, a bakery, a vet, a beauty shop, a swimming pool, and adventure!

Great Places to Visit!

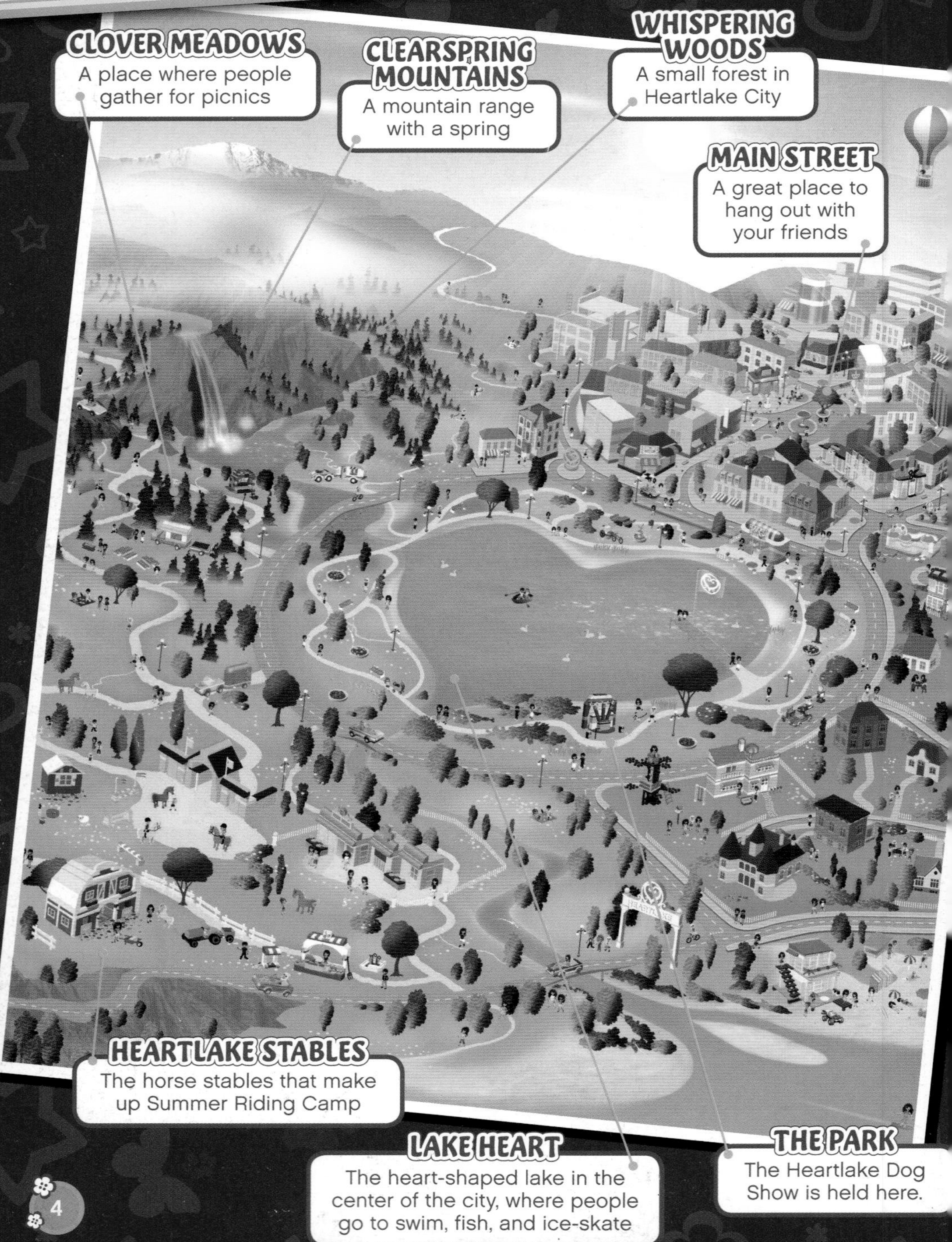
CLOVER MEADOWS
A place where people gather for picnics
CLEARSPRING MOUNTAINS
A mountain range with a spring
WHISPERING WOODS
A small forest in Heartlake City
MAIN STREET
A great place to hang out with your friends
HEARTLAKE STABLES
The horse stables that make up Summer Riding Camp
LAKE HEART
The heart-shaped lake in the center of the city, where people go to swim, fish, and ice-skate
THE PARK
The Heartlake Dog Show is held here.

HEARTLAKE HIGH

The local school attended by Andrea, Emma, Mia, Stephanie, and Olivia, and all of their friends

LIGHTHOUSE ISLAND

An island off the coast of Heartlake City

THE BEACH

The coastline. Emma and Olivia live near here.

Andrea

The performer of the group, Andrea is a talented singer and is great at making up her own songs. She loves anything that relates to music: singing, playing the piano, dancing, and the theater. She is a great cook and works at a café. She also has a not-so-secret love of bunnies.

Emma

Emma is an artist and loves being creative. She enjoys interior design, taking photographs, and making jewelry. She's also a fan of horseback jumping and karate. She is sometimes forgetful, but she's a wonderful friend.

Mia

The animal lover of the group, Mia enjoys spending time with lots and lots of animals. If she's not training animals, then she's probably taking care of them. She also excels at sports, skateboarding, and playing the drums. In her free time, she rides horses, goes camping, and practices magic tricks.

Olivia

Olivia loves science, nature, and history. If she could, she would spend all day inventing new things, as well as taking pictures and drawing. Super-intelligent and focused, Olivia is quite a brain. She's still clumsy sometimes, but who isn't?

Stephanie

A confident natural leader, Stephanie is very social, creative, and organized. She loves planning events, parties, and soccer. She enjoys talking to people, writing stories, and dancing ballet. Though at times a little bossy, she is very down-to-earth.

A Pop Star Comes to Town!

Chirp!
I'm so excited! I can't believe the big pop star Livi is in Heartlake City.
She's signing autographs at the mall today. There is even a rumor about a surprise performance!
CAFÉ
I absolutely love Livi! I'm so excited we're all going.
Andrea's still working, but she told us to go without her. She plans to meet us right after her shift is over.
A FEW HOURS LATER...
Huh? Who is that girl with all the security?
Welcome to the Café. What can I get you?
A Himalayan gemstone mineral water. But not too cold, please.
I'm sorry, we don't have that.
What a pity! That's my favorite water.
Well, then I'll have a decaf soy cappuccino with vanilla flavoring.

She's a strange one, isn't she?
I thought so too at first. But the way she's all covered up, and those bodyguards...I think she might be Livi.
Here's your cappuccino. Enjoy.
Thank you.
Have a nice day.
Keep the change.
Er, that's way too much for the coffee.
I think that *was* Livi! What an exciting way to end my shift. See you later.
Have fun!
Beep!
Where are U? Waiting for you!

There you are! Livi just started signing. But look how long the line is!
Her hands are going to be exhausted in no time.
I hope we get her autograph!
Phew, this is taking ages.
And she's due to perform soon. It's going to be close!
Sorry, everyone. We have to end the autograph session now. Livi will be presenting her latest song in half an hour.
Oh no! That can't be true!
Then all that waiting was for nothing?! Urgh!
Relax, girls! Maybe we can get our autographs after all.
What are you talking about?

Thanks to my job in the mall I know my way around here pretty well. I think I know where Livi's dressing room is.
Well, then, let's move! Now!
This should be it...
Oh, uh...excuse me, I think this is the wrong place.
Not quite what we were looking for, tee-hee!
Munch

Don't look at me like that! I can be wrong sometimes too. This is sure to be—
CRASH!
Ouch!
Switch the light on!
Stephanie! Are you all right?
Would someone help me out of here?
Ha-ha-ha! I didn't know you were on a treasure hunt!
BUT STEPHANIE DOESN'T GIVE UP.
The dressing room has to be here! Livi will be performing in 20 minutes!
You really know your way around here, don't you, Stephanie?! Maybe the janitor will be kind enough to give us an autograph.
Hey, I recognize him...Something tells me that this bodyguard will lead us straight to Livi. Follow me, girls!

What do we do now: knock?
Why don't you try your luck one more time, Stephanie!
Me? No way!
Excuse me...
Hey, what are you doing here? Out, right now!
I'm sorry for barging in. I wanted to thank you for the big tip earlier at the Café.
Wait, Karl! Such polite fans deserve a friendlier welcome.
We don't want to keep you long. But we would really like an...er...autograph. Please!
Thank you *soooo* much!!!
Anyone else?
Yes, please!
It's a good thing you followed your instincts, Andrea!
And thanks for being so brave. Without you we would still be standing here tomorrow.
That is *sooo* true. But let's go, girls! We don't want to miss Livi's first Heartlake City performance!
End

Popular Women in Music, Part One

Ella Fitzgerald

Ella Fitzgerald was one of the most popular female jazz singers of all time. Dubbed the "First Lady of Song," Ella was born in 1917 in Newport News, Virginia, but spent most of her life in New York. Ella Fitzgerald sang with the most notable jazz musicians of the twentieth century. Her recording of "A-Tisket, A-Tasket" topped the Billboard charts for seventeen weeks and sold over one million copies! At the very first-ever Grammy awards in 1959, Ella Fitzgerald went home with two Grammys! She made history by selling over 40 million albums and winning thirteen Grammy awards over the course of her career.

Kitty Wells

© Michael Ochs Archives/Getty Images

One pioneer in the country music scene was singer, songwriter, and musician Kitty Wells. Originally named Ellen Muriel Deason, Kitty was born in Nashville, Tennessee, in 1919. She was the first female vocalist to hit the country music charts. Some of her songs were catchy, others gave women a strong voice, and some did both. Kitty's success on the charts paved the way for many other female musicians. Kitty Wells was inducted into the Country Music Hall of Fame in 1976 and in 1991 took home the Grammy Lifetime Achievement Award.

Julie Andrews

Julie Andrews is best known for her famous movie roles in *Mary Poppins* and *The Sound of Music*. Born in Surrey, England, in 1935 as Julie Elizabeth Wells, Julie began her success on the stage performing in musicals. She is said by many to have one of the most beautiful voices ever heard and is known for having perfect pitch! She has been nominated for three Academy Awards, and won Best Actress in a Leading Role for *Mary Poppins* as well as a Grammy for the recordings from the movie. Her role in the musicals *My Fair Lady* and *Camelot* both earned her Tony Award nominations. In addition to being a singer and actress, Julie has also written several children's books! Julie Andrews has played some of the most important and groundbreaking female roles in history and continues to do so today. She was even given the incredibly special honor of being made a dame—which is the female equivalent of a knight!—by Queen Elizabeth II of England!

Aretha Franklin

Called the "Queen of Soul," singer, songwriter, and musician Aretha Franklin is so well-known that she's often referred to simply by her first name: Aretha. Born in 1942 in Memphis, Tennessee, Aretha began singing early and had already recorded some of her music by age fourteen! A gifted piano player as well as a talented vocalist, Aretha is mainly self-taught.

© Raymond Boyd/Michael Ochs Archives/Getty Images

Aretha is considered a strong African-American female icon and leader for young women in soul and rock-and-roll music. In 1987, she became the first female vocalist to be inducted into the Rock and Roll Hall of Fame. She has won eighteen Grammy Awards in her career, making her one of the most celebrated and successful female artists of her time. She is best known for her chart-topping success "Respect."

Barbra Streisand

Born in 1942 in Brooklyn, New York, Barbra Streisand is one of the highest-selling female recording artists of all time! She's an actress, singer, writer, composer, author, director, producer, designer, and more! She has won awards in almost every category imaginable, including Academy Awards, Tonys, Emmys, and Grammys. She began her career on Broadway. Her most famous role—*Funny Girl*—earned her a Tony Award nomination. She continued to appear in feature films and record albums, all of which were huge successes. Her debut as a director for the film *Yentl*, in which she also starred and sang, received five Academy Award nominations. Barbra Streisand is also known for her dedication to charity work, which includes tours, concerts, and benefits that have raised millions of dollars for worthy causes.

Patsy Cline

Patsy Cline was one of country music's top female stars and industry trailblazers. Born in Winchester, Virginia, in 1932 as Virginia Patterson Hensley, Patsy was said to have begun entertaining and singing for her neighbors at the age of three. She is considered to be the most popular female country music recording artist in history!

© Michael Ochs Archives/Getty Images

She's best known for her crossover smash hit "Crazy," which made both the top ten country and pop charts! Ten years after she passed away, she became the first female singer inducted into the Country Music Hall of Fame. Her stardom helped establish female singers as an integral part of the country-music scene, and her albums still sell to this day. In 1995, she was awarded the Grammy Lifetime Achievement Award.

Pop Stars are People Too!

MIA HAS A NEW JOB—SHE'S A DOG WALKER AT THE HEARTLAKE GRAND HOTEL. TODAY SHE'S EXTRA EXCITED BECAUSE SHE'S WALKING THE DALMATIAN PUPPY THAT BELONGS TO POP STAR LIVI!
Well, Cookie, what should we do? Throw sticks in the park?
Woof! Woof!
Cookie! What are you doing? Come back!
Cookie, no!— My apologies! I'm *sooo* sorry!
JUMP!
Whoa! Mia, it's me. Livi!
Oh, hello! Are you trying to get a bit of peace and quiet?
Exactly! But honestly, walking through the city isn't really relaxing!
I understand. I'm most relaxed when I'm riding my horse.
I used to ride too. But not since I got famous...
EVEN THOUGH MIA IS STARSTRUCK, SHE DECIDES NOT TO ACT ON IT. LIVI SEEMS A LITTLE LONELY. THIS GIVES MIA AN IDEA.

That's so sad! Come with me. We can go riding this afternoon!
Me? No! My manager, Megan, would never allow it.
It's far too dangerous!
What Megan doesn't know won't hurt her. Come on! *Pleeeease!*
Okay. Pick me up in an hour. But no one must see me!
It's been over an hour. I wonder if Livi bailed?
No, she'll be here. I won't give up on her.
There you are! In here!
Put these on. This way no one will recognize you!
This is great. Photographers have been following me all day.

Phew!
Now, let's go riding, Susanne!
Su—? Yes, hee-hee. I can't wait!
I can't believe that worked!
Not even your grandma would recognize you looking like that. Ha-ha!
It's so beautiful here. I'm already feeling better. You have no idea how hard it is to relax when paparazzi follow you everwhere.
This is my mare, Bella. And that beauty over there is Sunshine.
Whinny
Are you sure she'll like me?
Of course! She is totally gentle.
All right, then.

This is *sooo* lovely! I'm glad you talked me into joining you.
I always feel totally free when I'm out riding.
Exactly! Here I can completely be myself. Just me, not the pop star.
Ready to go faster?
You bet!
Yee-haw!
If you don't mind me saying it, you really should make more time to do stuff like this.
You're right. But life as a pop star is my dream. You can't have everything.
Yikes!
Plonk!
Argh!
SPLASH!

Did you hurt yourself?—Hey, what's that?!
Click! Click!
Oh no! A photographer!
Hey! Stop!
No way! These pictures are worth a fortune!
Whinny!
Mia, it's okay. Let him go.
No way! Some crummy photographer is not going to ruin this day.
I'M GONNA GET YOU!
Oh no! My camera got snagged!
Splash
Oh no! The smart card and the photos are ruined!
Sometimes life is fair after all.
I don't believe it. Talk about bad luck!
Drip
Drip
I'm sure Livi won't see it like that at all, hee-hee!

What am I going to tell Megan, Sunshine? The pictures will be on the Internet within the hour...
I don't think so. The photos were destroyed!
WHAT?! SERIOUSLY? That's amazing!
Is your happy dance going to last much longer or can we get riding again?
THE NEXT DAY.
What did you do yesterday, Mia?
I went riding with Livi.
I can prove it!
Yeah, sure. And I was on the moon, ha-ha!
Ha-ha-ha! Anyone can see that you photoshopped that picture.
Doh, you got me!
Phew, that was close! I almost revealed Livi's secret!
End

Women in Music, Part Two

Tina Turner

Pop star. Rock star. Movie star. Tina Turner is all three. At an early age, Tina was interested in the rhythm-and-blues sound that was popular in St. Louis. It wasn't long before she started performing, and quickly became known as an R&B legend. Tina's pop career soared in the 1980s, when she topped the charts with solo hits, one of which sold over twenty million copies! Tina's performance style is full of energy and pizzazz, and people love seeing her live. By the mid 1980s, Tina had hit the big screen in feature films and become a household name. In 1991, Tina was inducted into the Rock and Roll Hall of Fame.

© JStone/Shutterstock.com

Patti LaBelle

Known as the "Godmother of Soul," Patti LaBelle was born in 1944. She began her career singing in a group called the Bluebelles, who were known around the New York club circuit and performed regularly at the famous Apollo Theater. Later, they became the first African-American vocal group to make the cover of *Rolling Stone* magazine! Patti's solo career took off in 1984 with several hits. By 1986, she had a number one album and another number one hit song. She has been nominated for eleven Grammy awards—of which she has won two—been inducted into the Grammy Hall of Fame, and given a star on the Hollywood Walk of Fame.

Pat Benatar

Pat Benatar became famous in the 1980s as a real rock-and-roll star, and she maintains that status to this day. A singer, songwriter, and guitarist, Pat paved her road to stardom not by being a vocalist or pop star, but by producing hard-core rock with an edge. Born in 1953 in Brooklyn, New York, Pat didn't start pursuing her dream of being in a rock band until 1973. Her debut album came out in 1979 and included two huge hits that topped the charts. For over a decade, Pat dominated the rock scene as one of its leading female icons. She has ten platinum albums, four Grammy Awards, and eight number one singles under her belt!

© Everett Collection/Shutterstock.com

Janet Jackson

Originally known for being Michael Jackson's younger sister, Janet Jackson stepped onto the stage

© Everett Collection/Shutterstock.com

and into the solo spotlight in the 1980s. She soon garnered her own acclaim as one of the best-selling female pop stars of the twentieth century. The singer, songwriter, and actress was born in 1966 in Gary, Indiana. As a young child, she appeared in several popular television shows, solidifying her talent and interest in acting, which would reappear later on in life. She released her debut album in 1982, and it was a hit! Following that, she released several other albums, all of which included hits that topped the charts. Janet's album *Rhythm Nation 1814* produced seven top-five Billboard hits. She was the first artist in history to have done this with one album! She went on to star in many movies, and she received an Academy Award nomination for the song "Again," which she wrote for the film *Poetic Justice*. Janet remains a pop legend with albums that have sold millions of copies and changed the face of pop music.

Celine Dion

Celine Dion is a singer-songwriter and is one of the highest-earning musicians of all time! Born in Quebec, Canada, in 1968, Celine had already become a popular French recording artist by the time she was eighteen years old. She reached stardom in America after recording the theme song to the Disney movie *Beauty and the Beast*, which came in at number nine on the Billboard charts and won her both a Grammy and an Academy Award. Celine is perhaps best known for her blockbuster hit "My Heart Will Go On," which was the theme song of the popular movie *Titanic*, which won eleven Academy Awards, including for Best Song! Celine still performs to sold-out stadiums across the world and is considered one of the most popular performers in the history of pop music.

Selena

Selena Quintanilla-Pérez had many talents. Born in 1971 in Lake Jackson, Texas, Selena quickly became famous as a singer, songwriter, spokesperson, actress, and fashion designer. Known simply as Selena, she was referred to by many as the "Queen of Tejano Music," which is a type of Latin music that was very popular in Texas and Mexico. Selena won a Grammy in 1993 for her album *Live*. Aside from music, Selena was very active in her community and donated her time to important causes. This, along with her many contributions to music and fashion, made her one of the most celebrated Mexican-American entertainers of the late twentieth century.

Madonna

© yakub88/Shutterstock.com

Born Madonna Louise Ciccone, a young girl dreamed of one day being a star. And she did just that, becoming a singer, songwriter, actress, and businesswoman. She is often referred to as the "Queen of Pop"—a title she has earned by selling more than 300 million records worldwide. She is recognized as the best-selling female rock artist of the twentieth century, has won hundreds of music awards (including seven Grammys), and also won a Golden Globe for Best Actress in *Evita*.

Hair Color Hijinks

EMMA WORKS AT THE PET SALON IN THE AFTERNOONS. AS AN ANIMAL LOVER, IT'S A FUN WAY TO MAKE A LITTLE EXTRA POCKET MONEY.
Please be very careful with my sweetie, won't you?
Of course, Mrs. Noble. Cindy will love her new style. Won't you, Cindy?
I guess that means yes, tee-hee!
Lick!
Sweetheart, what a pretty dog you are!
Woof! Woof!
Ta-da, all pink and shiny!
Look what Mommy bought you!
How cute! A neckerchief that matches yours!

AS EMMA IS CLOSING THE STORE, STEPHANIE DROPS BY TO PICK HER UP.
Wow, someone's in a super mood!
My dance teacher played all of Livi's biggest hits.
Do you like her last album or her new album more?
They're both so good, I can't choose.
Um, do you really want to go out like that?
Why? What's the matter?
Oops! Pretty messy from training.
No problem, I'll give your hair a quick wash!
Really? While you're fixing my hair, could you make me look like Livi?
I'd be happy to!

Just enjoy your free head massage and relax.
Hmm, the perfect treatment after a dance class!
Huh. I hope I'm doing this right...
Wow, this feels like heaven...
AAAAAAHHHHH!!!
You said you wanted to look like Livi, so I gave you pink hair.
I was kidding! My parents are going to be so mad!
Oh no! It's not permanent color, but let's fix it anyway.
Gasp!
Don't worry! I can do this.
Hmm, where did I get this from?
EMMAAAA!
LATER...
NOOOOOOOOO!
Um, you don't like your hair blue and curly?

I look like I'm from another planet!
This will definitely get it out. I promise!
Woo-hoo, it worked! It's blond again!
Phew, thank goodness!
Yeeeah!
Yippie!
Hey, is this a hair salon party I didn't know about?
Well, it sure was a colorful hustle and bustle!
Wow! Have you done something with your hair? It looks great!
Don't ask!
Tee-hee!
End

Musician Fashion Stories

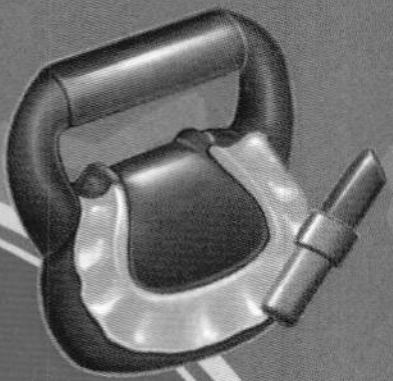

Being a musician isn't just about writing or recording great songs anymore—it's also about putting on a spectacular show. After all, musicians *are* performers too! Over the years, pop stars have influenced the face of fashion in many ways as they've worked with fashion designers, costumers, and even artists to create the perfect "looks" for their pop star personas.

Check out four of the most well-known fashion outfits made famous by female pop stars!

The Tuxedo

© Everett Collection/Shutterstock.com

A female star (and her two group-mates) made fashion history in 1969 when they performed on a popular nighttime variety show in head-to-toe black tuxedos with bow ties, top hats, and canes! They sure made a splash on camera that night.

© Salim October/Shutterstock.com

The Headdress

One popular actress and pop star made herself known for her spectacular—and gigantic—headdresses, which she wore regularly, on stage and off. Red sequins, white feathers, and bejeweled from head to toe, these headdresses were so monumental that they sometimes appeared larger than the star herself!

The Rock-and-Roll Look

© Inga Dudkina/Shutterstock.com

In the early 1980s, women rock-and-roll stars were very popular. One famous guitarist created a signature look—wild, short hair; ripped T-shirts; lots of black leather; and dark, smoky eye makeup.

The Swan Dress

© Everett Collection/Shutterstock.com

One female vocalist showed up at the Academy Awards in a white feather dress designed to look like a swan! Complete with swooping swan neck, face, and beak, this dress is considered one of the most iconic red carpet looks of all time!

A Creepy Costume Party!

Thank you! Have fun with the costume.
FOR HALLOWEEN, LIVI THROWS A SPOOKY COSTUME CONCERT AT THE MALL, AND SHE'S INVITED ALL THE FRIENDS. ANDREA VOLUNTEERED TO HELP OUT AT THE COSTUME SHOP SO SHE COULD GET A GREAT OUTFIT IN EXCHANGE.
The costume is great! I'll look really cool in it tonight.
Riiiing!
Hello! Can I help you?
Strange! Why is he running away?

ON HER LUNCH BREAK, ANDREA WALKS THROUGH THE MALL TO GET LUNCH AND CHECK OUT THE DECORATIONS
French fries and a lemonade. I'm looking forward to that!
Tapp! Tapp!
BUT SHE KEEPS HEARING FOOTSTEPS BEHIND HER.
Is someone there? Strange, I don't see anybody.
Why do I feel like I'm being followed? Halloween is starting to creep me out. Why is that vampire starting at me?
Oh no! It's that scarecrow again!
Wait a minute. It's Halloween, and hundreds of people are coming in costume for Livi's party tonight.
Cafe
No one is following me—I'm just being silly. I need to calm down

ANDREA IS JUST FEELING NORMAL AGAIN WHEN HER SUPERVISOR ARRIVES.
Hi, Mark!
Hi, Andrea! I just wanted to ask you to be particularly alert today.
Some of the staff noticed two characters in disguise who are lurking around in a suspicious way.
You mean a vampire and a scarecrow?
Yes! Have you seen them too?
Yes, unfortunately!
Take it easy, Andrea. If you see them, just call me.
Riiiing!
Hi, Andrea! Ready for the party?
What's up? You look like you've seen a ghost!
More like a vampire and a scarecrow.

ANDREA TELLS HER FRIENDS ABOUT HER CREEPY ENCOUNTERS.

...Thank goodness I'm finishing work now!
It is kinda creepy! No wonder you're scared!
Oh, don't be silly! Today is Halloween. I'm sure it's just a prank!
Do you really think so?
Maybe?
Is that one of them?
YEEESS!!!
Come on, let's follow him!
Are you serious?
Sure, it's the only way to find out what's going on.

There he is. Step on it, girls!
Drat, we lost him.
Over there! The scarecrow!
Stop, we just want to ask you a question!
He simply vanished!
Unbelievable...
What if they're **REAL** ghosts?
Look!
Over there!
But how? I don't believe it!
You two go that way, and I'll circle around this way.
We'll get them this time!
No sign of either of them!
Missed them again!
Seriously?!

Yikes, look at the time! The party is about to start!
Mia and Olivia will be waiting by now.
We have to get you changed first!
You're practically unrecognizable!
Just this wart, then you're done!
Totally cool! Thanks for the makeup job, Emma!
No problem! Now let's get off to the party!
BY THE TIME THE THREE FRIENDS ARRIVE, THE PARTY IS ALREADY IN FULL SWING
I think Livi is on next after this band.
I could use some water before we start dancing.
Me too. Playing ghost hunter is thirsty work!

Where have Olivia and Mia got to?
They should have arrived ages ago.
I don't believe it! What are THEY doing here?
Giggle! Hee-hee!
They're coming toward us!

What's up, Andrea? Didn't you recognize us?
This morning you said you would see straight through any disguise!
So we thought we'd put you to the test...
...and play a little Halloween trick on you.
Oh boy, you sure did a good job!
So you really didn't recognize us?
No! I guess I was showing off a bit too much this morning...
You should have seen your face!
Hee-hee-hee!
You can say that again!
You two are hilarious. Let's go dance!
AS THE FIVE FRIENDS LAUGH ABOUT THE DAY, LIVI COMES ONSTAGE. ANDREA'S NO LONGER SCARED—INSTEAD, SHE'S HAVING THE BEST TIME OF HER LIFE!
Cool!
Woo-hooo!
End

What's Your Music Fashion Style?

Imagine you're just like Livi—a global music sensation. Take this quiz and find out what your music fashion style would be!

1. You're on tour again. Tonight you're performing center stage in New York City! What are you going to wear?

A. Something amazing with sequins and jewels. Or maybe a long gown and a tiara. Or maybe I'll come out covered in Christmas lights. Who knows?!

B. Probably something with jeans and an old vintage or torn-up T-shirt. Your look is your look.

C. No matter where you are, you like to wear something that reminds you of home.

D. Comfortable and easy. Maybe some sweatpants and a really sporty top.

2. Today you don't have to perform at any music venues, so you can hang out with your friends. What are you going to do with your day?

A. Catch up on TV and movies with friends. Maybe a popcorn-and-pizza slumber party!

B. You and your pets need some quality time… on your motorcycle!

C. Something low-key. Maybe have a picnic outdoors and going horseback riding after.

D. Go to an old record store and look for rare, vintage albums.

3. You're making a fun music video with your friends. What are you going to do with your hair and makeup?

A. Something really fun and new—maybe you'll dress up like an old-movie starlet or an Egyptian queen. It depends on the video!

B Mohawk all the way!

C. Nothing too flashy. You like to keep it natural.

D. Probably a bright neon wig and some glow-in-the-dark makeup!

4. What's your favorite thing to wear on your feet?

A. Fun shoes with lots of color and design. Maybe sandals!

B. Black leather boots. Or maybe bare feet!

C. Cowboy boots!

D. Any sport or tennis shoe.

5. **What do you think is most important when it comes to your personal fashion style?**

A. Your stylist helps you with the latest trends, and you always look fashionable. But mostly, you like to have fun.

B. Really standing out. It's fun to be unique.

C. Something comfortable and flowing, like a nice dress or a good pair of denim jeans.

D Something you can dance in.

6. **You can sing, but can you also play an instrument? If so, which would be your favorite?**

A. You leave the instruments to your bandmates. You like to concentrate on singing and putting on an exciting show!

B. Maybe an electric guitar...and the drums!

C. Acoustic guitar. (Or maybe a banjo!)

D. All you need is a computer and headphones!

Write down the letters from your answers. Did you get more of one letter than the others? If so, then see what describes you best on the next page.

You chose mostly *A*'s:

You're a **Pop Princess** all the way! You love fashion and music, and your stylist keeps you up on the latest trends. Still, despite your princess status, you like dressing up ***and*** down—you always pick the perfect outfit for the perfect occasion.

You chose mostly *B*'s:

Watch out—you're a total **Rocker Girl!** You don't really care what day it is or what occasion you have to go to, you pretty much always look cool—it's your signature look. The best part? You always look like you. You look great, but you always do it your own way.

You chose mostly *C*'s:

Someone is a **Country Gal!** You have a wonderful small-town vibe about you, and your music is always heartfelt. You would rather top the charts with your homegrown vocals and laid-back style. You rather be comfortable than flashy! You might even know how to two-step!

You chose mostly *D*'s:

You're a **World-Famous DJ!** You know how to mix music on your computer, and you like to make some good beats to dance to. You and your friends love remixes of all the songs you hear on the radio. You and your friends also have a lot of energy, so it's good to wear something relaxed and easy.

You chose a little bit of everything:

Sounds like you might be daring and eccentric and willing to try any new look. This means you have range and like to have fun with style!

A Difficult Situation!

Hi, guys! Are you ready?
Ready? For what?
We're having our picnic today at Heart Lake with Livi! You forgot about it, didn't you?
Sorry, we've been super-distracted by the school magazine.
I thought it was tomorrow!
We have to jazz up the website.
So what's the big deal?
We have to figure out a way to keep reader interest. What we need is a really big story...
I've got it! We can do a story on Livi! We'll call it "The Secret Life of a Pop Star!"
Ahem! I don't like how you use Livi's friendship.
Maybe you're right...let's not do it.

LATER THAT AFTERNOON.
Hey, Livi! Here we are!
Sorry, I'm late. Rehearsals can take forever.
Hey, Cookie, come here!
Cookie, don't! I'm so sorry, Andrea!
It's okay!
Ha-ha! Cookie really seems to like Andrea!
Where did you get Cookie, Livi?
I used to work in an animal shelter.
I've always loved animals. And one day Cookie arrived there.
I knew he was my dog as soon as I saw a spot shaped like a music note in his fur.
It was fate!
I knew it! Super stories like this could save our website!

THE FRIENDS HAVE PLANNED SOMETHING VERY SPECIAL FOR LIVI.
Swan boats?! I've never seen anything like that before! They're amazing!
Splish!
Splash!
Wow, you're easily impressed!
That's because a pedal boat is something special for me!
I never have time for things like this.
But your life is much cooler!
Traveling from city to city and sitting around on my own in hotels isn't that cool, you know...
So what do you do when you have time off?
I really like reading. In every city, I go to a bookstore and buy myself a book.
I love to collect books from all over the world. That way, I remember all the fantastic places I've been.
ARGH! Another great story...which I *can't* tell!

Let's change places. I want to pedal too.
Sure!
Oh, these stupid mosquitoes! Get away from my nose!
Andrea, be careful!
Hold on! I've got you!
AAHHH!
Livi—the lifesaver!
Another great story!
Could you please stop that whispering all the time?!
What's up?
Those two are determined to put Livi's stories on their website.

Really? I think that's wrong. She's telling us these things because we're her friends.
We're not going to use the stories! Stop accusing us!
What's the matter? Are you arguing?!
Oh, nothing... We just...
Oh, okay...Our website doesn't have enough readers. So we thought we might write something about you...
But we're not going to! We don't want to take advantage of you!
Oh, guys! It's so great to have friends like you!
Huh?!
I'm always reading some nonsense about myself. I think it would be great if you wrote something that's true for a change!
Seriously?!

Seriously! It's really nice that you're so concerned about me.
That's great of you! Thank you!
Then let's get started right now: photo shoot in the swan boat! Ha-ha!
And then we'll take a photo of Cookie and me.
A LITTLE LATER.
It's sweet of you to want to protect me, Mia. The press isn't so considerate.
It's just that our friendship is important to me.
Ha-ha, the dog knows what's good to eat!
Stop, Cookie! That's my sausage!
THE ARTICLE ON THE WEBSITE IS ALSO A COMPLETE SUCCESS!
Did you read the article about Livi?! Can you believe she's here in Heartlake City?
And look at these pictures of her dog. He's so cute!
End

Elizabeth I, Queen of England...and Musician!

Elizabeth I was queen of England and Ireland from 1558 until she died in 1603. During her reign—known as the Elizabethan Era—music became an integral part of the English kingdom, culture, and society. She was well-known as a patron of the arts. She often threw banquets, at which there was always music, dancing, and theatrical performances. But did you know that the queen of England was also an accomplished musician?

© Everett Historical/Shutterstock.com

Queen Elizabeth played several instruments, including the lute (a stringed instrument like the guitar) and the virginal (a kind of keyboard that is part of the harpsichord family of instruments). The queen also had her own company of performers, the Queen's Players, who would perform for her regularly. Elizabeth also loved dancing! She encouraged dancing at every party and banquet she held at the palace and felt that dancing was wonderful and important exercise.

Because of Elizabeth's affinity for music, noblemen were expected to know how to play the lute and sing well enough to accompany any ensemble. During her years as queen, she encouraged all musicians and composers, and employed many musicians in her kingdom. Her love of the musical arts also led to a wider business of musicians purchasing published musical compositions to play. And, as the ability to play an instrument was an official skill required by the queen's court, English schools and universities began to teach music to their students. This is a main reason why music is still so important in our classrooms today!

The Big Concert!

This is the best day of my entire life!
Super!
Encore!
Bravo!
TWO WEEKS EARLIER...
Just you and *meee*, and you will *seee*, *thaaat's* what friends are *foooor!*
LIVI'S CONCERT AGENCY IS RAFFLING OFF A DUET WITH LIVI. NATURALLY, ANDREA IS DESPERATE TO WIN IT.
That was great, Andrea!
That was awful. The plant can sing better than me!
Nonsense! This will blow Livi away! You're guaranteed to win the competition!
Do you really think so?
YES! Your voice is amazing, and you've always dreamed of an opportunity like this. Just believe in yourself!
Gosh, I'm so excited!

Then send the video off. Now!
All right, all right, I will.
Right. Now let's keep our fingers crossed!
Done!
THE DAYS GO BY WITHOUT ANYONE CONTACTING ANDREA.
The concert is coming up fast, and I haven't heard anything. I guess someone else must have won. Wait...I think my phone is ringing.
Rrrring rrring
Yes, Andrea speaking!
REALLY?! I won?! Yes, of course, I'm interested!
Splash!

NATURALLY, ANDREA TAKES HER FRIENDS WITH HER TO THE CONCERT.
I'm so excited! Do you think the audience will like me?
Of course they will!
Do you like my Livi fan wig? All the super-fans are wearing one today.
I think you really look like Livi!
Hm, not sure if anyone other than Livi can pull this color off...
There you are at last!
Uh—what?!
It's my first day on the job, so your styling and makeup need to be perfect!
Huh?—But, wait...
Dust
I'm not Li—UMPF!!!
Will you keep still, Livi?!

Hey, guys! They think Olivia is Livi!
Ha-ha-ha! That's hilarious!
Well, any minute now they're going to realize that it isn't her.
There's been a mistake...
You're right. Your lipstick should be brighter.
Okay, honey, here we go.
Wait a minute! I'm not...
Wow, that's quite a hairdo! Ha-ha!
OOOOOOOHHHHHH!
WOOOSH
WOOOOSH
Shouldn't we help Olivia, guys?
Just wait a little longer— at some point they'll figure it out.

What?! Honestly, I'm not...
Quick, put this on, honey!
Livi! What happened? That dress fit perfectly yesterday!
That's because I'm not Livi!
You see! The misunderstanding is cleared up already.
You're such a joker, Livi! Incredible!
That's enough!
Ha-ha-ha!
Oh no, they don't believe her. We have to help!
Are you coming to the photo shoot, Livi?
Steph! Do something!

HEY! Didn't anybody notice that I wasn't here?
Um, what...?!
Hi...
Livi! Where did you come from?
Hmpf...
I was locked in the bathroom for over an hour, and no one noticed.
Then it wasn't you at all...?!
I kept telling them I wasn't you! Livi, please, don't be mad. It was all a misunderstanding...
Oh boy, she is really angry!
I'm not going on stage with her! She'll eat me alive!

My dear Livi, I heard about the broken door. You were trapped, you poor thing!
Yeah, for a whole hour!
Calm down, honey. You have to get ready for the concert! Okay?
Okay...
THE FRIENDS ARE ALLOWED TO WATCH THE CONCERT IN THE VIP AREA.
Wow, I didn't think that Livi would be so angry!
I'd be mad too if no one noticed I'd been missing for an hour!
I thought she was going to throw us straight out!
Livi's not like that. She knows it wasn't our fault.
Still!— I don't want to perform with her anymore. I'm too nervous!
Don't be nervous. You're going to do great. You've been practicing for days.
Yes! Stay strong! Today is YOUR day!

Boy, can she sing!
Totally awesome!
Andrea? It's time to head backstage.
I'm sorry for behaving the way I did! I'm always *sooo* nervous before performances. I hope you can understand!
Of course I can! Wow, I never thought stars like you get nervous too!
That's absolutely normal; we're all just humans after all! Just take a deep breath, and together we're gonna rock this place!
Thank you!
AND LIVI WAS RIGHT!
Encore!
Bravo!
End

Putting on a Show!

Being a pop star is hard work and so is putting on a concert! Ever thought of putting together your own big show? Here are some things to for you and your friends to consider beforehand.

Location, Location, Location!

Picking your venue is very important. Consider the space you'll need, how public or private it is, and how much foot traffic you'll get. Figure out how much seating you need and what the acoustics are—you want to sound good, don't you? Whether you choose your living room, the local library, or even the sidewalk in front of your school, make sure you get permission first. It's always good to have your parents help out too!

Tickets!

Pick a date for your show and make sure you've given yourself enough time to get ready. You want people to come, right? Then, make sure to give them advance notice when you invite them. Send an invitation with all the details, including location, time, and, of course, price of admission! Remember, free tickets always get the biggest crowds.

Design Your Concert

Choose a theme for your show, and make sure your songs, costumes, and set designs all work around this theme. When you have something special tying everything together, the outcome is so much more professional—and emotional!

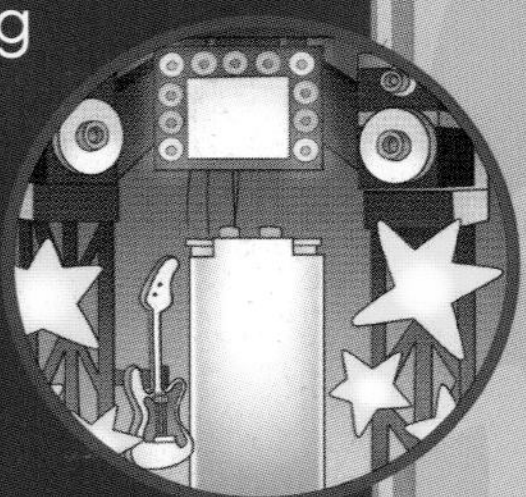

Practice Makes Perfect

If you want to put on a good show, you're going to need to practice. Make sure you're putting in the time you need to make your show great. Know the words, the song list, and, of course—your dance moves! Perhaps ask a parent to help plan.

Getting Ready

Feeling nervous before a show is perfectly normal. But there are some things to do that will help you be your best: Sleep well the night before your show. Have one or two extra practices in the morning. And make sure to eat and drink pretty of fluids before the show. You want to make sure you have all the energy you need!

A New Home

It's a pity your tour is finished.
When are you going back home?
I'm not. I decided to stay in Heartlake City for a while.
Seriously?
That's great!
HURRAY!!!
Won't it be a bit boring for you here?
Not at all. Touring is exhausting! I could really do with a nice break.
You see, I want to write my next songs myself. And I need peace and quiet for that.

Hmm...but I have no idea where I'm gonna stay.
I know! You could rent a suite in my auntie's hotel!
Let's go there now!
Great idea! I'd have plenty of room there and wouldn't have to take care of everything.
Hi, Aunt Susan! Can we take a look at the suite?
Hello! Er...what?
It would be great advertising for the hotel if a star lived here.
That's true. But let's see whether Livi likes this room first.
I like it a lot! I'll take it!
Yippee!
Sign here, Livi. Once your luggage arrives, I'll have it taken to your new room.
Scribble
Awesome!

A FEW DAYS LATER.
Hi, Livi. You look sad—what's wrong?
My things still aren't here. Could you please check with Aunt Susan?
Pst, Andrea!
Yes. What's up?
Livi's things were delivered this morning.
Huh? So where are they, then?
Nate was supposed to take them to the suite.
Nate the bellboy?! Uh-oh! He can be so clumsy and forgetful!
You have to find Livi's things. Quickly!
I'll turn the whole hotel upside down if I have to. I need to fix this, and fast!

Nothing here, either! I just don't believe it!
What am I supposed to tell Livi? "Sorry, we've lost all your things"?—Huh?!
Oh no! Those are Livi's things!
I'm so sorry! Clearly, the boxes were delivered to the wrong room.
Oh, I see! I was wondering what I could wear this dress with. Ha-ha-ha!
ANDREA CAN'T DO IT BY HERSELF, SO SHE CALLS IN HELP FROM HER FRIENDS.
Hurry up!
All the boxes have to be in Livi's suite before she notices anything!
Phew, they're so heavy!
My things are here. Great!
PHEW!
Er, yes...just arrived, hee-hee!

THE NEXT DAY.
Zzzzz
Hmmm...How about that?...No, that doesn't work, either!
Oh, Cookie! Writing song lyrics isn't easy. Maybe I'm not a real artist after all...
What am I doing here?
I think I'd better go home and carry on as before...
Hello-o! Are we interrupting anything?
No, no! I'm just feeling a bit desperate.
Why?
I'm trying to write a song, but I can't think of anything good to write about!
You just need to take a break.
Nonsense! You need some inspiration!
They're both right.
You need a break AND some inspiration...
...and I know just the place.

ONLY A LITTLE LATER...
Wow, it's so cool here!
SURPRISE!
Isn't it perfect for coming up with new ideas?
CLANK!
To new ideas!
It's fabulous here! Oh, look what Cookie's found!
We call her "Jojo." She's totally tame. Come and see!
Oh, she's so cute!

BACK WITH THE OTHER FRIENDS...
Food always helps when you're down.
Right. I LOVE grilling food over a campfire.
Me too! But I also love sweets. As a kid I always used to steal them in the shop...
Blow
...but it's not what you think! My parents own the candy store I took from, and they always caught me.
Seriously? Cool, you grew up in the land of milk and honey!
You were lucky! My mom wanted me to eat vegetables all the time!
Yes, but then you always took all my sweets.
Hey, I didn't eat all that many!
YES, YOU DID!
How long have you guys been friends?
Since the first day I moved to Heartlake City.

Wow, that's amazing!
Don't you miss your friends?
Yes, sometimes. And my parents too, of course.
If you're feeling lonely, we're always here for you. You know that, right?
You guys are really great!
That's what friends are for. To friendship!
To friendship!
Exactly, friendship! I think I've just found something to write my first song about.
End

LEGO Friends
LEGO Friends
Adventures in Heartlake City
BONUS PAGES! Maps! Activities! Stories! And more friendship fun!
LEGO Friends
Friends to the Rescue!
BONUS PAGES! Maps! Activities! Stories! And more friendship fun!
Don't miss out on all the fun... Build your friendship library!